Discovering Tyrannosaurus Rex

Written by Rena Korb
Illustrated by Ted Dawson

Content Consultant:
Kenneth Carpenter
Curator of Lower Vertebrate Paleontology & Chief Preparator
Denver Museum of Nature and Science

visit us at www.abdopublishing.com

Published by Magic Wagon, a division of the ABDO Publishing Group, 8000 West 78th Street, Edina, Minnesota 55439.
Copyright © 2008 by Abdo Consulting Group, Inc. International copyrights reserved in all countries. All rights reserved.
No part of this book may be reproduced in any form without written permission from the publisher.

Looking Glass Library™ is a trademark and logo of Magic Wagon.

Printed in the United States.

Text by Rena Korb
Illustrations by Ted Dawson
Edited by Jill Sherman
Interior layout and design by Emily Love
Cover design by Emily Love

Library of Congress Cataloging-in-Publication Data
Korb, Rena B.
  Discovering Tyrannosaurus rex / Rena Korb ; illustrated by Ted Dawson ; content consultant, Kenneth Carpenter.
     p. cm. — (Dinosaur digs)
  ISBN 978-1-60270-109-0
  1. Tyrannosaurus rex—Juvenile literature. I. Dawson, Ted, 1966- ill. II. Title.
QE862.S3K6735 2008
567.912'9—dc22
                              2007034046

FOSSIL FINDS

In 1902, dinosaur hunter Barnum Brown made an amazing discovery in Montana. He found the fossil of an enormous dinosaur—the biggest meat eater that had ever been found. Henry Field Osborn, a paleontologist at the American Museum, gave the dinosaur the name *Tyrannosaurus rex* (tuh-RA-nuh-sor-uhs reks). Over the next few years, Brown found two more *T. rex* fossils in Montana, including the first skull. It was almost four feet (1 m) long with eight-inch (20-cm) teeth.

In 1990, the largest, most complete *T. rex* was found in South Dakota. It is called Sue, not because it was a female, but because Susan Hendrickson discovered the fossil. Sue was not only the largest *T. rex* ever found, it also contained more bones than other *T. rex* fossils. These bones allowed paleontologists to learn more about *T. rex*.

Hong kicked his feet against the rocky ground. He had been in Montana for two weeks, searching for dinosaur fossils with his father and his father's students. They hoped to find one of the scariest dinosaurs ever, *Tyrannosaurus rex*.

Even though he was only nine years old, Hong had read a lot about *T. rex*. He knew that *T. rex* stood on two legs with its tail held out behind it. He knew that its head might be four feet (1 m) or more long and its jaws were filled with a mouthful of terrifyingly long teeth.

Hong had seen *T. rex* teeth before. They were the size and shape of a banana. Millions of years after dinosaurs disappeared from Earth, the teeth remained sharp.

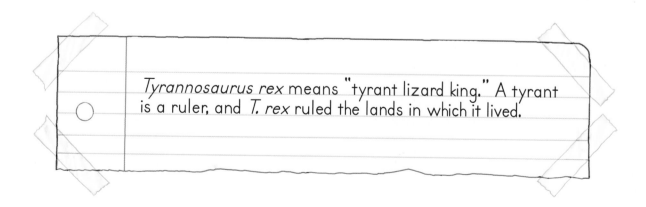

Tyrannosaurus rex means "tyrant lizard king." A tyrant is a ruler, and *T. rex* ruled the lands in which it lived.

Hong also learned about dinosaurs from going on digs with his father, a paleontologist. Hong's father studied ancient forms of life and taught about them at a college. During the summer, his father always went on digs. Sometimes, he traveled as far away as South America or Mongolia. This summer, he had brought his students and Hong to Montana.

Hong knew that many fossils had been found in Montana. The area was a good place to find *T. rex* fossils. *T. rex* only lived in western North America. Paleontologists, fossil collectors, and even high school students have discovered fossils in Montana, Wyoming, South Dakota, Colorado, Utah, New Mexico, and Canada. But so far, Hong's group had found nothing.

Hong's father and his students gathered to study their maps. They wanted to know where *T. rex* already had been found. That might tell them the best place to search.

"Dad," Hong called, "I'm going for a walk."

His father nodded. As long as Hong did not go too far, he was allowed to explore. Hong followed a dry creek bed that took him farther and farther away from the group.

T. rex stretched about 40 feet (12 m) long and weighed about 12,000 pounds (5,400 kg). The height at its hips was 13 feet (4 m) tall—that is 3 feet (1 m) taller than a basketball hoop!

Hong spied a small hill and decided to climb up and get a better view. Sixty-five million years ago, *T. rex* ruled this land. Back then, the area was woodland, filled with trees. Now, as far as he could see, cliffs poked high into the sky. The ground was covered with rock, dirt, and scruffy yellow and green grass.

Somewhere beneath that ground might be a *T. rex*. If only they knew where to look!

Hong was about to hike down the hill when he noticed something sticking out from the ground. At first, it looked like brown rocks. But Hong was not fooled. He knew that rocks in Montana were tan or gray, not brown.

Hong bent down and took a closer look. What he saw made him run back to his father as fast as he could!

The only *T. rex* footprint ever found was in New Mexico. The footprint was almost three feet (1 m) long and showed that *T. rex* had large claws.

Soon enough, Hong's father was nodding in agreement. Hong had discovered a dinosaur bone! The bone was covered with a thin coat of dirt. Hong's father brushed away some of the dirt.

He stepped back so everyone could see. "This is the arm bone of a dinosaur," he told them. "What else can we learn from looking at this bone?"

For a long time, *T. rex* was thought to be the largest meat-eating dinosaur. But now paleontologists know that *Giganotosaurus* and *Carcharodontosaurus* were even bigger.

Hong studied the bone carefully. "The bone is thin," he said. "It also has layers like an onion."

"And what does that mean?" Hong's father prodded.

"*T. rex* was a very big dinosaur with layered bones!" exclaimed Hong.

"I think Hong has discovered our *T. rex*," announced Hong's father.

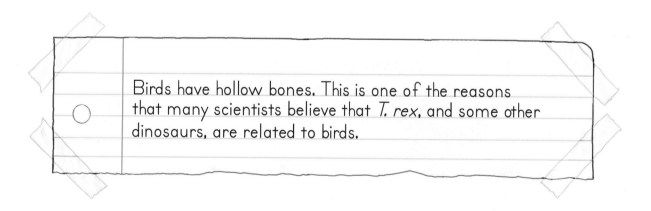

Birds have hollow bones. This is one of the reasons that many scientists believe that *T. rex*, and some other dinosaurs, are related to birds.

The team found another bone next to the arm bone. This bone went back into the hard rock. The team would have to dig through the rock in order to uncover it.

Wearing goggles and gloves for protection, they used jackhammers to break up the hard rock. Then, they used crowbars to roll the rock out of the way.

All their hard work paid off. Soon, more bones became visible. The team worked even harder to uncover these bones.

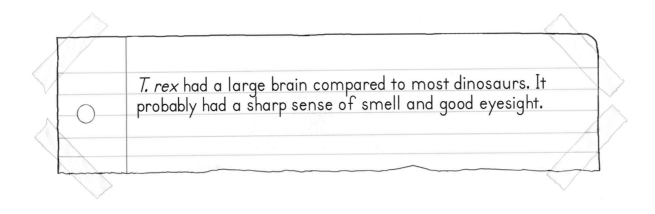

T. rex had a large brain compared to most dinosaurs. It probably had a sharp sense of smell and good eyesight.

Now that the bones were visible, the team began to carefully clear away some of the dirt. Hong worked beside his father. They used trowels to remove the dirt and awls to scrape it away from the bone.

"Do you remember why we use such small tools?" Hong's father asked him.

Hong rolled his eyes. The question was too easy. "Big tools can hit the bones," he explained. "We want to be sure to keep the bones in one piece."

Soon, the shape of the *T. rex* peeped through the rock and dirt. Hong could see the dinosaur, from its huge skull down to the tip of its long tail.

Hong stared at the powerful jaw and the teeth that were serrated like a saw. These teeth were meant for eating meat. *T. rex* may have used its sharp teeth to attack living dinosaurs, eat the bodies of dead dinosaurs, or both.

Hong had read that *T. rex* could crunch through bone with its powerful jaw. Now he saw just how easy that would be!

Teeth were very important for survival of *T. rex* and other dinosaurs. If a tooth got chipped off or pulled out in a fight, a new tooth would grow back.

Before removing any bones, everyone worked to draw a map of how the animal lay. Hong knew mapping was very important. The position of the bones could tell paleontologists about how the animal died and what bones were connected.

Hong carefully drew the bones that made up part of an arm. The arms of a *T. rex* were too short to reach its mouth, but they were very strong. They were about as long as a man's arms but three times as thick.

Once the team had finished the map, it was time to take out the bones. First, they divided the dig site into sections that would get packed together. Then, they covered the sections in wet newspaper. Next, they soaked burlap strips in plaster. They wrapped these strips over the newspaper, just like wrapping a bandage around a sprained ankle. When the plaster dried, the bones on the inside were safe and protected.

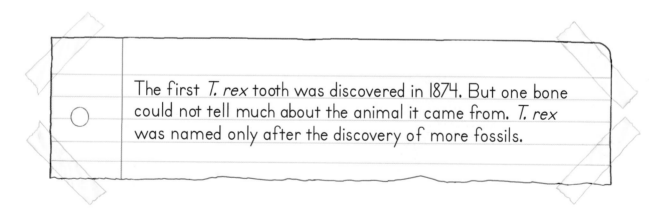

The first *T. rex* tooth was discovered in 1874. But one bone could not tell much about the animal it came from. *T. rex* was named only after the discovery of more fossils.

Finally, they loaded up the trucks to haul the bones away. Hong watched the trucks leave. He felt happy and sad at the same time. He knew he would not see his *T. rex* for a long time.

But one day, after the bones were cleaned and put back together, Hong would go see the *T. rex* in a museum. And he would know that he had helped bring this wonderful creature to the surface for all to see.

ACTIVITY: Tools for Digging

What does a paleontologist use these tools for?

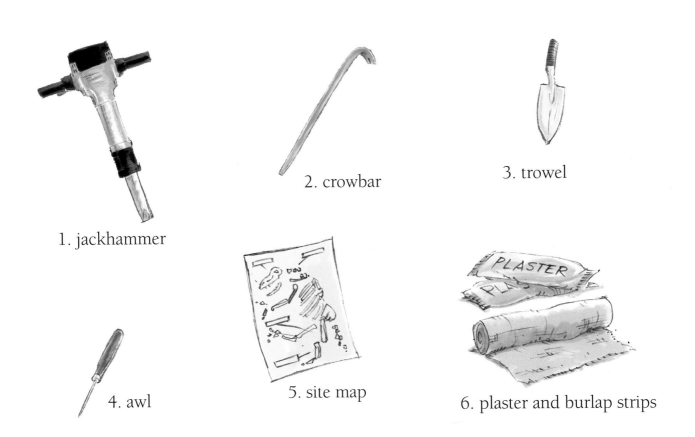

1. jackhammer

2. crowbar

3. trowel

4. awl

5. site map

6. plaster and burlap strips

ANSWERS:
1. to break up hard rock; 2. to roll rock out of the way; 3. to remove dirt from bones; 4. to scrape away dirt from bones; 5. to tell paleontologists how the bones were laying; 6. to wrap up bones for moving

GLOSSARY

awl — a tool with a sharp point.

dig — a place where scientists try to recover buried objects by digging.

fossil — the remains of an animal or a plant from a past age, such as a skeleton or a footprint, that has been preserved in the earth or a rock.

paleontologist — (pay-lee-ahn-TAH-luh-jist) a person who studies fossils and ancient animals and plants.

serrated — with small V-shaped teeth along the edge, like a saw.

trowel — a small handheld tool with a curved scoop for lifting plants or the earth.

woodland — land that is covered with trees, shrubs, or bushes.

READING LIST

Holtz, Dr. Thomas R., Jr. *T. Rex: Hunter or Scavenger?* New York: Random House Books for Young Readers, 2003.

Landau, Elaine. *Tyrannosaurus rex.* New York: Children's Press, 2007.

Schomp, Virginia. *Tyrannosaurus and Other Giant Meat-eaters.* Tarrytown, NY: Marshall Cavendish, 2003.

Zoehfeld, Kathleen Weidner. *Terrible Tyrannosaurs.* New York: HarperCollins Publishers, 2001.

ON THE WEB

To learn more about *Tyrannosaurus rex*, visit ABDO Publishing Company on the World Wide Web at **www.abdopublishing.com**. Web sites about *Tyrannosaurus rex* are featured on our Book Links page. These links are routinely monitored and updated to provide the most current information available.